REFRAME

Connecting Faith & Life

LEADER GUIDE

W9-BTS-944

REFRAME LEADER GUIDE
COPYRIGHT ©2014 REGENT COLLEGE

All rights reserved worldwide. No part of this publication may be reproduced, distributed, sold or licensed without the express written consent of Regent College with the sole exception that use of electronic and physical copies of the material are permitted for use by individuals participating in an authorized *ReFrame* discussion group.

Written by *Adam Joyce*
Produced by *Russell Pinson*
Edited by *Kate Harris, Mark Mayhew, and Ceri Rees*
Graphic Design and Layout by *Free Agency Creative*

PUBLISHED 2014 BY
Regent College Publishing for the *Regent College Marketplace Institute*
marketplace.regent-college.edu

IN ASSOCIATION WITH
The Washington Institute for Faith, Vocation & Culture
washingtoninst.org

REGENT COLLEGE PUBLISHING
5800 University Blvd, Vancouver BC V6T 2E4 Canada
regentpublishing.com
info@regentpublishing.com

Scriptures taken from THE HOLY BIBLE, NEW INTERNATIONAL VERSION®, NIV® Copyright © 1973, 1978, 1984, 2011 by Biblica, Inc.™ Used by permission. All rights reserved worldwide. New International Version" and "NIV" are registered trademarks of Biblica, Inc.®. Used with permission.

Extracts from The Book of Common Prayer, the rights in which are vested in the Crown, are reproduced by permission of the Crown's patentee, Cambridge University Press.

ISBN 978-1-57383-515-2

Cataloguing in Publication information is on file at Library and Archives Canada.

Table of Contents

Introduction

Welcome to ReFrame—a film-based
discipleship resource that explores how to
connect faith with all of life. Developed by
Regent College's Marketplace Institute, in
association with the Washington Institute
for Faith, Vocation and Culture, ReFrame
integrates Regent College's graduate
curriculum with stories, questions, and
exercises to engage the complexity of our
daily experience.

Concept

Many Christians today experience a frustrating and confusing disconnect between the story of Scripture and the story of our lives. ReFrame begins with the conviction that the story of Scripture is relevant to all of life: our jobs, our responsibilities, our relationships, and our world.

ReFrame equips Christians from all areas of life—scientists, artists, homemakers, politicians, janitors, engineers, farmers, everyone—to make this connection. The goal of ReFrame is to help Christians see the gospel with fresh eyes and experience the renewing power of Jesus Christ in every aspect of their lives.

"I can only answer the question 'What am I to do?' if I can answer the prior question 'Of what story or stories do I find myself a part?'"

–Alasdair MacIntyre

Stories matter because they frame how we see and live in the world. We are surrounded by a multitude of cultural stories trying to tell us who we are and how we should live. The story of Scripture is often viewed as irrelevant—disconnected from the difficulties, questions, joys, and sorrows of life. It's easy for Christians to conform to the pattern of this world (Romans 12:2) and lose sight of the true story.

Drawing from the experience of the disciples on the Emmaus road (Luke 24:13-35), ReFrame encourages a transformation of how we understand and live our own stories. The course invites participants to *encounter* Jesus in their everyday circumstances, *understand* the meaning of Jesus' life and work in the Biblical story, and *respond* to Jesus in practical and creative ways.

ReFrame invites you to re-encounter the truth of Jesus and the Scriptures. Our hope and prayer is that your eyes will be opened to see Jesus afresh, and that you will be filled with confidence and joy to live every aspect of your life fully for him.

Approach

ReFrame is an interactive 10-session course that invites engagement with deep theological teaching in the context of our own stories and life experiences. Designed for groups of about six to twelve adults together with a leader, ReFrame follows a three-part structure over the course of its ten sessions.

Part 1: The Story We Find Ourselves In

Sessions 1-2 introduce ReFrame and our cultural context.

Part 2: The Story of Scripture

Sessions 3-7 focus on knowing the biblical story and how it reframes our perspective of God and ourselves.

Part 3: The Ongoing Story

Sessions 8-10 focus on how God calls us to respond to the biblical story in the midst of our own stories, and invite us to be ambassadors to the culture around us.

Note: while relevant to many contexts, ReFrame primarily engages a Western cultural context and heritage.

Format

Sessions follow a standard two-hour template, which can be adjusted by the leader as necessary.

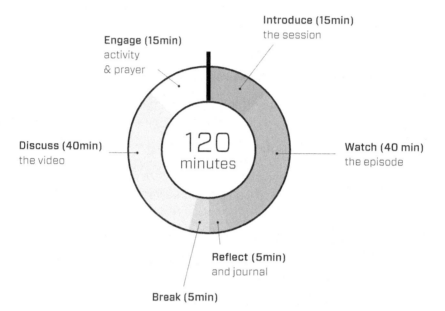

Introduce (15min)
the session

Engage (15min)
activity
& prayer

Discuss (40min)
the video

120
minutes

Watch (40 min)
the episode

Reflect (5min)
and journal

Break (5min)

INTRODUCE THE SESSION

Each session begins with a recap of the previous session and a reflection question. The central topic of the session is then introduced, along with a Scripture passage to read aloud. You'll then enter into a short time of prayer before beginning the video.

WATCH THE EPISODE

Each 40-minute ReFrame episode is a mixture of talks, interviews, and stories all related to the central topic of the session. A professor from Regent College provides a talk, which is interspersed with commentary from evangelical thought leaders. Ordinary people also share their experiences of how the full narrative of Scripture has impacted their personal story. Outlines of each episode's central topics are provided in the guides, together with space for your own notes.

REFLECT AND JOURNAL

This portion of ReFrame is a devotional and reflective space, where participants are invited to discern what God is saying to them through a time of silence, prayer, and journaling. It draws on the story of the disciples on the Emmaus road (Luke 24:13-35) and is designed to create space for participants to encounter Jesus. If appropriate for your group, participants may be invited to share their reflections together. Space is provided within the guide for journaling, with additional space for notes and reflection in the back. Participants may also wish to bring their own journals.

DISCUSS THE EPISODE

Questions are provided for the group to discuss the main themes of the episode. The goal of this time is to deepen understanding, so don't feel pressured to cover everything. If you are having trouble getting the conversation going, consider asking one or more of the following:

· What was new or significant for you?

· What did you find helpful?

· Were you surprised by anything?

· Was anything confusing?

· What questions were raised for you?

· Was there anything that specifically connected with your life?

ENGAGE THROUGH ACTIVITY AND PRAYER

Each session is designed to be self-contained, with no preparation required of the participants. However, every session includes an activity, some of which can be completed during the session itself, while others are optional and can be completed before the next session. Where activities are optional, spend the time explaining the activity and answering any questions the participants may have.

The sessions end with an invitation to pray together about the key themes and any specific prayer requests that arise. In addition, a historical prayer is provided as a reminder of the church's rich heritage and as an encouragement for us today. The prayers are collected in the *Prayers Throughout the Ages* segment in the back of the guide.

FURTHER RESOURCES

Each session includes a list of recommended resources to develop your thinking further. Introductory material is listed first, moving towards more advanced content. Additional resources can be found at *reframecourse.com*

LEADER PREPARATION AND NOTES

A preparation list for the leader is provided for each session. Also, Leader's Notes (LN) are provided throughout the guide on the left hand side of the page.

Alternative Formats

Not every group can meet for two hours, so as the leader, feel free to adjust as necessary. Include the portions you think are most relevant and valuable, for example:

60 Minutes		90 Minutes	
40 min	Watch	5 min	Introduce
15 min	Discuss	40 min	Watch
5 min	Pray	5 min	Reflect
		30 min	Discuss
		10 min	Engage & Pray

ReFrame can also be run in different group formats. Watch episodes in a large gathering and then sub-divide into smaller discussion groups, or run the whole session within a standard smaller group setting.

Tips for Leading ReFrame

Pray: Pray for your group and your time together.

Prepare: Get ready for each session by watching the video beforehand and preparing for the activity as necessary. Notes to help you prepare are provided at the beginning of each session.

Modify: Every group is different. The standard time (two hours) and group size (6-12 participants) are recommendations. Adjust both of these as you see fit.

Focus: Try to keep the session and discussion tightly focused. Use the recap and intro to focus the group but don't get stuck here, try to get to the video within the time suggested.

Conversation: As a leader, facilitating conversation is a big part of your role. You do not have to have all the answers, but rather help people engage and wrestle with their questions. Life is complex and so is living out God's story, so avoid easy answers.

Questions: You do not have to cover all the questions for each session. Feel free to follow people's curiosity and the questions that naturally emerge.

Listen: Every good conversation involves listening. Guide the *discussion* and help participants listen well to one another. Remind the participants that they are all encouraged to contribute each week.

Hospitality: ReFrame tries to follow the natural rhythms of a group: time to gather, connect, discuss, reflect, and take breaks. The typical two-hour model does not include space for a meal, although feel free to provide refreshments. Set aside additional time to share a meal together if you wish.

Further Questions: Visit *reframecourse.com* for more tips.

ReFrame Sessions

Part 1: The Story We Find Ourselves In

The Reframing Story

PREPARE

- *Supplies:* Large sheet of paper, individual sheets of paper (one for each participant), or a white board

- Review Session 1 Leader Guide

- Watch the episode and take note of points relevant for the discussion

- Pray for your group's time together

- Have a Bible on hand

"The truth of the story Jesus told was clear to the disciples because it made sense of everything."

-Paul Williams

 15 min

LN Allow time for each participant to introduce their name, where they are from, their occupation, and something fun or unusual about themselves. If everyone knows each other already, share something surprising people won't already know.

LN When you have finished the group introductions, introduce the central topic for this session, and invite someone to read Colossians 1:16-20.

Overview

INTRODUCTION

If Jesus is the redeemer of all things, how does faith reframe every aspect of our lives? How does Christianity connect to the whole of who we are? Is Jesus relevant in an increasingly complex world? These are the types of questions many of us wrestle with today.

ReFrame aims to help you live out your faith in everyday life, encouraging us to encounter Jesus afresh and allowing his story to shape our own. This first session explores how a fragmented and complex world can tempt Christians to either withdraw from, or assimilate to, the culture around them. However, the true story of Jesus enables Christians to resist these temptations and to live integrated and faithful lives.
Read Colossians 1:16-20.

LN Pray for your time together and then begin the video.

40min

Episode Outline & Notes

Complexity—Modern life is getting more complex and fragmented.

Integration—We experience competing cultural messages and can find it difficult to integrate life and faith.

Assimilate or Withdraw—The complexity and challenge of living out our faith tempts Christians to assimilate or withdraw.

Example of Emmaus—Knowing the biblical story and being shaped by it helps us live integrated and authentic lives.

Jesus—The true story of Jesus makes sense of everything, bringing meaning and purpose to all of life.

 5 min

Emmaus Road Reflection

LN Read Luke 24:15.

"As they talked and discussed these things with each other, Jesus himself came up and walked along with them." Luke 24:15

LN Spend five minutes in silence, praying and reflecting on the questions provided. Remind participants there is additional space in the back of the guide.

What has God been saying to me through this episode (e.g. encouragement, challenge)?

What was significant or new? What questions did it raise?

Where is your Emmaus Road? Where are you in your journey of discipleship with Christ? Where do you want to see more of Jesus in your life?

LN After this reflection time, allow for a 5-minute break. If appropriate, invite participants to share their reflections.

 **40 min**

LN Invite participants to discuss and apply the main themes of the episode together. Don't feel pressured to cover everything. The goal of this time is to deepen understanding. If the discussion is slow getting started, try asking some of the example questions from the Introduction.

"The call of the Gospel, the claims of God and the lordship of Christ in our lives has to do with all of who we are."

—**Ruth Padilla DeBorst**

Discussion

What types of complexity and fragmentation characterize modern life? In what ways are our lives becoming more or less complicated?

What are some areas of life that Christians struggle to connect with their faith?

What questions are you currently wrestling with? What do you hope to learn from ReFrame?

Further Resources

The Insect and the Buffalo by Roshan Allpress and Andrew Shamy

The Drama of Scripture: Finding Our Place in the Biblical Story by Craig Bartholomew and Michael Goheen

The Gospel in a Pluralist Society by Lesslie Newbigin

For additional resources go to reframecourse.com

15 min

Engage

ACTIVITY

Our faith in Christ means something for every aspect of our lives. However, sometimes it is still difficult to see Jesus in the different places we find ourselves. Think about the past week. Call to mind some of the different places, activities, and situations you were involved in. Where did you see Jesus? Where did you feel his presence? Where did you not feel connected to him? Be concrete in your examples.

"A story can do so much more than just teach you. It can transform you."

–Sally Lloyd-Jones

LN Take a whiteboard or large sheet of paper. Draw a line down the middle, dividing it into two columns. At the top of one column, write, "Where we see Jesus" and for the other, "Where we struggle to see Jesus." Invite the group to fill in each column. If you do not have a large sheet of paper, have each individual draw these columns on their own sheet of paper, fill them in, and then share back with the group.

LN When the group has provided a number of examples, cross out the line in the middle and draw a large circle around all the examples. Explain that this is what ReFrame hopes to help Christians do—to see Jesus in all of life.

LN Recall from the discussion time the specific questions, hopes or goals the group has for ReFrame. Pray about these requests and ask God to help you encounter Christ in every aspect of life. End your time by saying together the prayer for this session.

PRAY

Leader to life, Path to truth, our Lord Jesus Christ; you led Joseph to Egypt, and the people of Israel through the Red Sea; and Moses to Mount Sinai, and his people to the land of promise. And you traveled with Cleopas and his companion to Emmaus. Now, I pray you, Lord lead me and my companions to travel in peace on the journey before us. Save us from the visible and invisible enemy and lead us safely to the place we are headed. For you are our way and our truth and our life. Glory and worship to you now and always and unto the ages of ages. Amen.
–Hovhannes Garnets'i

Part 1: The Story We Find Ourselves In

Cultural Stories

PREPARE

· Review Session 2 Leader Guide

· Watch the episode and take note of points relevant for the discussion

· Pray for your group's time together

· Have a Bible on hand

"One of the features of the postmodern world is the fluidity of its culture and therefore the fluidity of its identities."

–James Houston

 **15 min**

LN Allow for a brief time to connect and then invite the group to recall what ReFrame has covered up to this point.

Overview

RECAP

Last session explored how, in a complex world, it can be difficult to see how our faith connects with all of life. Instead of connecting our faith with all of life, we can be tempted to either assimilate or withdraw from the culture around us.

Since the last session, where have you experienced or noticed any examples of the temptation to either assimilate or withdraw?

LN As the recap reaches a natural lull, introduce today's session and then invite a participant to read Romans 12:1–2.

INTRODUCTION

Who am I? How does my faith in Jesus affect how I answer that question? How does our culture shape our response to this question of identity? Is there a conflict? As Christians, the story of Scripture and the person of Jesus shape the whole of who we are. And yet we often experience tension with our culture, which provides alternate answers to this question. We are told we must choose who we want to be, rather than receive our identity as a gift given by God.

LN Pray for your time together and begin the video.

This session discusses some of the ways our culture shapes us, and why this so often leads to a crisis of identity. **Read Romans 12:1–2.**

40min

Episode Outline & Notes

Key characteristics of our culture contribute to our contemporary identity crisis:

Dislocation—Tradition is treated with skepticism, which creates a break with the past. We're cut off both from our history and from the future.

Invention—Individuals have the right to choose who they want to be. We exercise this choice through consumption—buying and selling our identity.

Fluidity—Our identities are constantly changing in line with cultural trends and fashions. We constantly ask the question, "Who am I now?"

Constraint—Infinite choice at the personal level is held together by conformity at the public level. Our private and public lives are divided, creating a conflict between them.

 5 min

Emmaus Road Reflection

LN When the video has finished, read Luke 24:15.

"As they talked and discussed these things with each other, Jesus himself came up and walked along with them." Luke 24:15

LN Spend five minutes in silence, praying and reflecting on the questions provided. Remind participants there is additional space in the back of the guide.

What has God been saying to me through this episode (e.g. encouragement, challenge)?

What was significant or new? What questions did it raise?

LN After this reflection time, allow for a 5-minute break.

40 min

LN Discuss the main themes of the episode together. Don't feel pressured to cover everything. If conversation is slow to get going, ask a starter question: what was significant, helpful, or confusing for you? What questions did it raise?

"The question, 'Who am I?' gets settled once and for all in the statement, 'I AM.' We are, because he is."

–Sarah Williams

Discussion

What was Christine struggling with in how her identity was being shaped?

What are the cultural messages that try to shape who we are? What does culture tell us makes a happy and full life?

Where do you feel cultural pressures in your life?

What activities help you, or could help you, remember that your identity is rooted in Christ?

Further Resources

Counterfeit Gods by Timothy Keller

The Trouble with Paris by Mark Sayers

The Universe Next Door by James Sire

For additional resources go to reframecourse.com

15 min

Engage

ACTIVITY

We're surrounded by cultural messages that are trying to shape our identity (e.g. advertising, movies, workplaces). These messages have an underlying story about what it means to be a person—defined by what you do, or have, or feel. Part of connecting faith to all of life involves being aware of the patterns of the world around us, and in our own lives.

Next time, bring an example of something in your week that represents a cultural story about identity—positive or negative. This could be an advertisement, article, song, product, place, conversation or experience you had. Take a photo, bookmark a website, write down an idea, or bring something to share next time.

LN This is a recommended, not required, activity designed to help participants practice what we've discussed this session. Just like "show and tell," ask participants to bring in tangible examples of cultural stories.

PRAY

Lord, to be turned from you is to fall, to be turned to you is to rise, and to stand in you is to abide forever. Grant us in all our duties your help, in all our perplexities your guidance, in all our dangers your protection, and in all our sorrow your peace; through Jesus Christ our Lord.
–Augustine

LN Allow time for participants to respond in prayer. Pray specifically for God to help us draw our identity from Christ and set us free from false identities. Have a participant close your time with the prayer for this session.

Part 2: The Story of Scripture

Creation & Fall

PREPARE

- *Supplies:* Arrange some fresh coffee beans in the centre of your group

- Review Session 3 Leader Guide

- Watch the episode and take note of points relevant for the discussion

- Pray for your group's time together

- Have a Bible on hand

"When our relationships with God, creation and other humans are right, biblical faith proposes that all of God's creation will know *shalom*—a Hebrew word that means fullness of life, wellbeing."

-Iain Provan

 15 min

Overview

LN Allow for a brief time to connect and then invite the group to recall what you discussed in the previous sessions.

RECAP

Last session discussed how different aspects of our culture can confuse our answer to the question, "Who am I?" These cultural stories draw our gaze away from Jesus and lead to an identity crisis, creating confusion and frustration about who we are. By contrast, Sarah Williams argued that the question "Who am I?" is best answered by being rooted in the biblical story. It is only within this narrative that we meet the person of Jesus Christ and are able to rest confidently in our true identity.

LN Invite participants who completed the optional activity from the last session to share with the group (e.g. ads, movies, songs, experiences).

If you brought a tangible object, photo, link, or experience that serves as an example of underlying stories about identity, share it with the group.

How easy, or hard, was it to identify and evaluate the underlying stories?

LN As the recap reaches a natural lull, introduce today's session and invite a participant to read Genesis 1:1–5, 1:26–31.

INTRODUCTION

Over the next five sessions, we are going to cover the key moments in the scriptural story. This session starts with the beginning—the account of the creation and fall. Genesis tells us why God created the world and humanity, and his purposes for both. God's creation was good, but this goodness was catastrophically marred through the fall. As the image-bearers of God, we are nevertheless called to cultivate this nevertheless goodness in our relationships with God, others, and

LN Pray for your time together and then begin the video.

creation. **Read Genesis 1:1–5, 1:26–31.**

40min

Episode Outline & Notes

Temple—God created the cosmos and ordered it. The cosmos is like a sacred temple, but it is not itself divine.

Humanity—We are made in the image of God; humans are called to be kings (culture makers) and priests (cultural caretakers).

The Fall—The fall broke relationships, causing alienation and diminishing shalom (fullness of life), but does not negate the goodness of creation. In the brokenness of the world, God is working to redeem creation.

Vocation—We are invited to participate with God in this work of redemption. Shalom is restored in the cosmos through reconciled relationships with God, each other, and creation.

 5 min

Emmaus Road Reflection

LN When the video has finished, read Luke 24:15.

"As they talked and discussed these things with each other, Jesus himself came up and walked along with them." Luke 24:15

LN Spend five minutes in silence, praying and reflecting on the questions provided. Remind participants there is additional space in the back of the guide.

What has God been saying to me through this episode (e.g. encouragement, challenge)?

What was significant or new? What questions did it raise?

LN After this reflection time, allow for a 5-minute break.

40 min

LN Don't feel pressured to cover everything. If conversation is slow, ask a starter question: what was significant, helpful, or confusing for you? What questions did it raise?

"The biblical narrative helps us to understand that work itself has an inherent purpose, not just an instrumental purpose. The work itself matters."

–Amy Sherman

Discussion

What tension did Hugo struggle with? What was creating this tension?

What do Genesis 1 and 2 tell us about who we are and God's purposes for creation? What does the fall mean for God's original purposes?

How could remembering the beginning of the biblical story change how we think about our vocations and our culture?

Where do you experience tension between faith and other areas of life? Understanding the creation story helped resolve Hugo's tension, what difference might this make for the tensions you experience?

Further Resources

Every Good Endeavor by Timothy Keller and Katherine Leary Alsdorf

Culture Making by Andy Crouch

Seriously Dangerous Religion by Iain Provan

For additional resources go to reframecourse.com

 15 min

Engage

LN Place some coffee beans in the middle of the group, enough for a handful each, as a reminder of the goodness of creation. Invite participants to pick up a small handful and take them in with their senses: look, touch, smell. Imagine where the coffee bean might have come from and the process that brought it to your group.

ACTIVITY

Coffee beans provide a tactile reminder of God's good work of creation. Even though a raw coffee bean is good, you probably would not want to eat it. It requires work—roasting, grinding, and brewing—in order to turn it into coffee. Such work, the work of people like Hugo, echoes God's original work and is rightly called "good."

Recall those times when you've had good coffee with family and friends (or if you don't like coffee, remember when you've shared a good meal), when coffee has been a gift from God for enjoyment or for fostering friendship. The many moments of making and sustaining are part of everyone's vocation. Think about the times where God's good work of creation is reflected and continued through your work in the world.

LN Allow time for people to share matters for prayer arising from the session. Invite the group to pray that they would know more deeply how their passions, gifts and talents are part of their vocation as God's image-bearers, his kings and priests, in the world. Close with this prayer.

PRAY

Give us grace, O Lord, to work while it is day, fulfilling diligently and patiently whatever duty you appoint us to do; doing small things in the day of small things, and great labors if you summon us to any; rising and working, sitting still and suffering, according to thy word. Go with us, and we will go, but if you do not go with us, send us not; go before us, if you put us forth; let us hear thy voice when we follow. Hear us, we beseech you, for the glory of your great name.
–Christina Rossetti

Part 2: The Story of Scripture

Israel's Calling

PREPARE

- Review Session 4 Leader Guide
- Watch the episode and take note of points relevant for the discussion
- Pray for your group's time together
- Have a Bible on hand

"God has taken an ordinary people like Israel, like the church today, and has done extraordinary things not because we are extraordinary, but because he is an extraordinary God."

–Soong Chan-Rah

 15 min

Overview

RECAP

LN Allow for a brief time to connect and then invite the group to remember what you discussed in the previous sessions.

Last session explored the story of creation and our vocation as human beings. God's original creation was good, but this goodness became catastrophically marred through the fall. As the restored image-bearers of God, we are called to cultivate shalom as kings and priests in our relationships with God, others, and creation.

When this story is forgotten, we create a false sacred/secular divide between our faith and the rest of life. The true story, as John Dickson mentioned, is that "Everywhere we step is sacred. The fall does not negate the goodness of creation…. We will see glimpses of the good everywhere."

Since the last session, where have you seen "glimpses of the good" (e.g. home, workplace, community, culture, creation)?

INTRODUCTION

LN As the recap reaches a natural lull, introduce the session and invite a participant to read Genesis 12: 1–7.

This session focuses on God's faithfulness to the people of Israel, and how Israel's story is part of our family history as Christians. The story of Israel helps us see how our faith makes a difference in a complex and messy world. Indeed, God calls ordinary people to trust him and blesses them so that they might be a blessing to others. God is with us—in our failures and our faithfulness—and continues to work through us to redeem this broken world. **Read Genesis 12:1–7.**

LN Pray for your time together and then begin the video.

40min

Episode Outline & Notes

Abraham to David

Called to trust—God moves the story along by calling ordinary people to trust and obey.

Blessed to be a blessing—The people of Israel are to be God's redemptive agents, seeking shalom in every aspect of daily life and being a blessing to the world.

David to Exile

In exile, it looked like God had failed to keep his promises; but God keeps the story moving even when his people fail him.

Exile to Jesus

Against all expectations, God brings the story to a magnificent fulfillment in Jesus and promises to redeem all of creation.

 5 min

Emmaus Road Reflection

"As they talked and discussed these things with each other, Jesus himself came up and walked along with them." Luke 24:15

LN When the video has finished, read Luke 24:15.

What has God been saying to me through this episode (e.g. encouragement, challenge)?

LN Spend five minutes in silence, praying and reflecting on the questions provided. Remind participants there is additional space in the back of the guide.

What was significant or new? What questions did it raise?

LN After this reflection time, allow for a 5-minute break.

40 min

LN Don't feel pressured to cover everything. If conversation is slow, ask a starter question: what was significant, helpful, or confusing for you? What questions did it raise?

"One of the wonderful things to me about the Bible is that there really are no heroes .... The stories of Isaac, and Jacob, and Joseph and the brothers, they are all full of people like us that do stupid things and are still in the story. Nobody gets ejected."

–Eugene Peterson

Discussion

What struck you about Rich Dean's fear about working as a lawyer? What changed for him?

What was God's purpose in calling Israel? How did God work in the life of Israel and ordinary people?

Rich Dean faced complex situations. Are there situations or areas of life that are impossible to redeem? Should Christians be involved? Discuss why or why not.

What complex situations have you experienced? What can you learn from the story of God's relationship with Israel in these situations?

Further Resources

Story as Torah by Gordon J. Wenham

How to Read the Bible Book by Book by Gordon Fee and Douglas Stuart

The Mission of God: Unlocking the Bible's Grand Narrative by Christopher J.H. Wright

For additional resources go to reframecourse.com

15 min

LN This is a recommended, not a required activity, designed to help participants embody what we've been discussing. If participants are going to participate, ask them to consider sharing their experience with the group next time.

LN If appropriate, ask if anyone is facing a complex situation or struggling to trust God. Pray for them. Also pray for the activity; that everyone would have an opportunity to be a blessing to someone else. End by asking a participant to say this prayer.

Engage

ACTIVITY

God calls us, like Israel, to be a blessing to others through acts of everyday faithfulness.

Remember a time when someone helped you during a difficult time through an act of kindness. Or when someone blessed you with a simple gesture. What impact did this have on you? If appropriate, share this experience with the group.

Now think of someone you would like to encourage, either as a group or personally. It could be a friend, a family member, or a colleague. Before the next session, try to do something to encourage and bless them. This could involve taking the person out for a meal or coffee, or writing them a note. Tell them what you appreciate about them. Be specific in your encouragement.

PRAY

God, you called your servant Abraham from Ur in Chaldea, watching over him in all his wanderings, and guided the Hebrew people as they crossed the desert. Guide and guard us your children who, for the love of your name, journey through this life. Be our companion on the way, our guide at the crossroads, our strength in weariness, our defense in dangers, our shelter on the path, our shade in the heat, our light in the darkness, our comfort in discouragement; that through your guidance, we may arrive safely at the end of our journey and, enriched with grace and truth, may return to our homes filled with lasting joy.
–Codex Calixtinus

Part 2: The Story of Scripture

Jesus
the King

PREPARE

- *Supplies:* Provide an individual sheet of paper for each participant

- Review Session 5 Leader Guide

- Watch the episode and take note of points relevant for the discussion

- Pray for your group's time together

- Have a Bible on hand

"Jesus is more than a Saviour. Jesus is the King and he is creating a kingdom in which he is the ruler. That's the message of the story of the Bible—that God will dwell with us, through Jesus, so that we can become the people of God in this world."

-Scot McKnight

 15 min

LN Allow for a brief time to connect and then invite the group to recall what you discussed previously. If they are comfortable, invite participants who engaged in the optional activity to share their experience.

Overview

RECAP

Last session showed that the story of Israel is part of our family history as Christians. Throughout the history of Israel, God calls ordinary people to trust him and serve as his redemptive agents of blessing to the world. Even when we fail, God is faithful and continues to work through us and move creation's story to fulfillment in Christ. God's promise to Abraham was that he would make the Israelites "a great nation to be a blessing to all nations."

Since last time, how have others been a blessing to you through small acts of everyday faithfulness?

LN As the recap discussion reaches a natural lull, introduce the session and invite a participant to read John 1:1–18.

INTRODUCTION

This session focuses on Jesus Christ as the climax of the story—the fulfillment of all the Old Testament scriptures (Luke 24:27). He is the true image of God, and true Israelite, who redeems humanity through his person, work, and words. Jesus is both Saviour and Lord, and his redemptive work affects everything, which gives meaning to all of life and culture —including our ordinary activities. The gospel is therefore more than personal salvation; it is the invitation to participate in a renewed life for a renewed world. **Read John 1:1–18.**

LN Pray for your time together and then begin the video.

40min

Episode Outline & Notes

First century Israel—Israel returned from exile in Babylon, but after 400 years they are still waiting for God to restore Israel and free them from pagan rulers.

Messiah—Jesus fulfills the Old Testament expectation for a Messiah and a true king.

Mighty words and deeds—Jesus reveals what God is like, providing a renewed vision of what it means to be fully human.

Holiness—Holiness is not about a single moment of salvation, but a life engaged in people-keeping—acts of loving your neighbour.

 5 min

Emmaus Road Reflection

LN When the video has finished, read Luke 24:15.

"As they talked and discussed these things with each other, Jesus himself came up and walked along with them." Luke 24:15

LN Spend five minutes in silence, praying and reflecting on the questions provided. Remind participants there is additional space in the back of the guide.

What has God been saying to me through this episode (e.g. encouragement, challenge)?

What was significant or new? What questions did it raise?

LN After this reflection time, allow for a 5-minute break.

35 min

LN Don't feel pressured to cover everything. If conversation is slow, ask a starter question: what was significant, helpful, or confusing for you? What questions did it raise?

"Christ came to make us whole, restoring all the broken pieces, which means we can't isolate our Christianity out to the side."

–Mariam Kamell

Discussion

When you think about Jesus being part of the larger story of Scripture, how does it change the way you think about him and his life?

What difference does it make to recognize Jesus as both Saviour and King?

What does Jesus show us about what God is like? What does Jesus reveal about what it means to be human and what it means to be holy?

Further Resources

The King Jesus Gospel by Scot McKnight

Simply Jesus by N.T. Wright

Christ Plays in Ten Thousand Places by Eugene Peterson

For additional resources go to reframecourse.com

"What is our end, what is our purpose? Well our end, our purpose, is to be like Christ. We are made in the image and likeness of Christ."

–Hans Boersma

 **20 min**

LN This is a group "brainstorming" activity to help participants see their daily activities as contributing to the thriving of those around them. Ask an individual to share an activity they find difficult, and invite the group to imagine how it does or could connect with people-keeping–loving our neighbours.

LN Pray for God to open your imagination to see this week how your everyday activities are connected with Jesus. Also, allow time for specific prayer requests arising from this session. Invite a participant to close your time with the prayer for this session.

Engage

ACTIVITY

Jesus' lordship and redemptive work affects every aspect of our lives. Christine's understanding of her vocation was reframed when she connected her daily activities (at home, community, workplace) with Christ's calling to love others and help them thrive—"people-keeping" as Rikk Watts reminds us.

Write down the activities in your life that are easy to connect to people-keeping, the ones that contribute to the lives of others. Then write down an activity where it is difficult for you to see a contribution to the flourishing of others. If you're comfortable, share the activity you find difficult with the group. As a group, discuss how you might reframe this activity. How does it, or could it, be connected to people-keeping?

PRAY

Christ be with me, Christ within me,
Christ behind me, Christ before me,
Christ beside me, Christ to win me,
Christ to comfort and restore me,
Christ beneath me, Christ above me,
Christ in quiet, Christ in danger,
Christ in hearts of all that love me,
Christ in mouth of friend and stranger.
 –Patrick

Part 2: The Story of Scripture

New Heavens
& New Earth

PREPARE

- Review Session 6 Leader Guide
- Watch the episode and take note of points relevant for the discussion
- Pray for your group's time together
- Have a Bible on hand

"Every human being asks questions of eschatology, of what the future will be like. What we believe about the future actually affects the way that we live our lives now, which is why the language of a new heaven and new earth matters."

–Steve Garber

 **15 min**

LN Allow for a brief time to connect and then invite the group to recall what you discussed in the previous sessions.

Overview

RECAP

Last session discussed how Jesus is the climax of the story, the one who fulfills God's promises to Israel and changes everything as Saviour and Lord. Christ provides a renewed and full vision of what it means to be human, offering us a truly full life. Rikk Watts said, "Holiness is about people-keeping," pointing to how Christ calls us to embody neighbourly love in every area of life.

Since your last meeting, where in your own life have you observed examples of people-keeping? What about more broadly in your neighborhood, workplace, city, politics, locally, and globally?

LN As the recap reaches a natural lull, introduce the session and invite a participant to read Revelation 21:1–4.

LN Pray for your time together and then begin the video.

INTRODUCTION

This fourth scriptural segment looks at how God promises to transform all of creation in the new heavens and new earth through the resurrection of Christ. As citizens of this promise, Christians are called to be holy foretastes, living previews of this final act of redemption. **Read Revelation 21:1–4.**

40min

Episode Outline & Notes

The Resurrection—The resurrection is God's vindication of Jesus and an unexpected fulfillment of Israel's hopes.

Jesus' Resurrected Body—Jesus' resurrected body affirms the goodness of physical creation, acts as a sign of the new heavens and the new earth, and challenges misconceptions we may have about heaven.

New Heavens and New Earth—The resurrection points to the promise of cosmic shalom—the complete transformation and renewal of creation.

Citizens of Heaven—As citizens of heaven, we are to faithfully live out the story of Scripture as a sign and foretaste of this final restoration.

 5 min

LN When the video has
finished, read Luke 24:15.

LN Spend five minutes in
silence, praying and reflecting
on the questions provided.
Remind participants there is
additional space in the back
of the guide.

Emmaus Road Reflection

*"As they talked and discussed these things with each
other, Jesus himself came up and walked along with
them." Luke 24:15*

**What has God been saying to me through this episode
(e.g. encouragement, challenge)?**

**What was significant or new? What questions did
it raise?**

LN After this reflection time,
allow for a 5-minute break.

 **40 min**

LN Don't feel pressured to cover everything. If conversation is slow, ask a starter question: what was significant, helpful, or confusing for you? What questions did it raise?

"God's calling us to be people whose lives give to other people this foretaste of what is coming in the future kingdom. This is what God wants me to be. He wants me to be this foretaste bringer."

–Amy Sherman

Discussion

Why did Vincent feel so helpless? Where have you experienced a sense of hopelessness when seeing the brokenness of the world around us?

What are common cultural pictures of heaven? How do these pictures compare with Christ's resurrection and the promise of our own resurrection?

Was there anything from the session that was new, significant, or raised questions for you, related to your understanding of heaven?

How does the promise of the new heavens and the new earth make a difference today? How might it make a difference for what we do now?

Further Resources

Surprised by Hope by N.T. Wright

When the Kings Come Marching In by Richard Mouw

The Great Divorce by C.S. Lewis

For additional resources go to reframecourse.com

 **15 min**

Engage

ACTIVITY

We live between Jesus' resurrection and the promise of new heavens and new earth; the Kingdom is here but not fully. This means we experience tension—difficult moments when we encounter the world as it was not meant to be. However, God promises that our labour is not in vain and Jesus' resurrection is God's ultimate commitment to restore all of his creation and dwell with us.

The prayer below is an expression of hope, a testament that God will use our lives, vocations and occupations to witness for Christ and redeem a broken world—even if we can't see that today.

Before the next session use this prayer to pray for the brokenness around you: a difficult job situation, a hurting friend or colleague, a struggling neighbourhood, broken institutions and systems in our society and world. Remember God's resurrection promise that through Christ, everything will be made new. Consider saying this prayer in those places of brokenness, or as you begin each day.

PRAY

God of heaven and earth, we pray for your kingdom to come, for your will to be done on earth as it is in heaven. Teach us to see our vocations and occupations as woven into your work in the world. We ask for your great mercy, for ourselves and those around us. Give us eyes to see that our work is holy to you, O Lord, even as our worship is holy to you. In the name of the Father, Son and Holy Spirit. Amen.
–Steven Garber

"One of the things Iranaeus said was that the glory of God is a human being fully alive. I think that that's a profound truth."

–J.I. Packer

LN If appropriate, ask if anyone wants to share any specific area of their life, or a situation locally or globally, where they struggle to maintain hope but want to see more of God's Kingdom to come. Pray for these situations as a group, or in pair, and invite a participant to close your time with the prayer for this session.

Adapted from *Visions of Vocation* by Steven Garber. Copyright (c) 2014 by Steven Garber. Used by permission of InterVarsity Press, P.O. Box 1400, Downers Grove, IL 60515, USA. www.ivpress.com

Part 2: The Story of Scripture

The Church
& The Spirit

PREPARE

- *Supplies:* Have one large candle, a lighter, and a small candle for each participant (e.g., a tea candle)

- Review Session 7 Leader Guide

- Watch the episode and take note of points relevant for the discussion

- Pray for your group's time together

- Have a Bible on hand

> "The descent of the Holy Spirit at Pentecost means that we can never be mere spectators in God's story. We are participants."
>
> **–Bruce Hindmarsh**

 15 min

LN Allow for a brief time to connect and then invite the group to remember what you discussed in the previous sessions.

Overview

RECAP

Over the last four sessions, we have explored the story of Scripture—the story of God's work to redeem people and creation. Last time we considered the completion of this redemptive work, and how the resurrection of Christ is a sign of God's promise to transform all of creation in the new heavens and new earth. As citizens of this promise, Christians are called to live as a sign, a holy foretaste of this final act of redemption.

If you prayed for God's "kingdom to come" since the last session, where did you pray? What did you ask for God to heal? What, if anything, did you see differently as you prayed?

LN As the recap discussion reaches a natural lull, introduce this session and then invite someone to read Acts 2:1-4.

LN Pray for your time together and then begin the video.

INTRODUCTION

How do we enter into the story? In this final session on Scripture's story, we see how at Pentecost, God gives the Holy Spirit to empower the church. It is not enough to simply know the story; we must also live the story. The Holy Spirit empowers us to participate in the story and God's work of redemption in the world. **Read Acts 2:1-4**

40min

Episode Outline & Notes

Participants—The Holy Spirit makes it possible for us to be more than observers or spectators of the story.

Renewed—The Spirit gives us a renewed mind, a renewed life, and adopts us into the triune family of God.

The Church—Just as Jesus ascends and the Spirit descends, the church also moves in two directions—the Spirit binds Christians together and missionally sends them out.

Continuation—The Spirit moves the story through the centuries and across geographies.

 5 min

LN When the video has
finished, read Luke 24:15.

LN Spend five minutes in
silence, praying and reflecting
on the questions provided.
Remind participants there is
additional space in the back
of the guide.

Emmaus Road Reflection

*"As they talked and discussed these things with each
other, Jesus himself came up and walked along with
them." Luke 24:15*

**What has God been saying to me through this episode
(e.g. encouragement, challenge)?**

**What was significant or new? What questions did
it raise?**

LN After this reflection time,
allow for a 5-minute break.

35 min

LN Don't feel pressured to cover everything. If conversation is slow, ask a starter question: what was significant, helpful, or confusing for you? What questions did it raise?

"We work with God in the church to build up the body of Christ and then we have the scattered church and we carry the gospel— we carry justice, we carry shalom into the world, participating with God in his work in the world."

–Ross Hastings

Discussion

What did Mary struggle with? What changed for her?

When have you felt you went from being a spectator to being a participant—from just knowing about the Biblical story to being "pulled through the frame"?

Why was Pentecost significant for the early church? What is the role of the Holy Spirit in the early church and today?

What is your experience of the Holy Spirit? How vital is life in the Spirit for living the Christian life?

Further Resources

Keep in Step with the Spirit by J.I. Packer

Missional God, Missional Church by Ross Hastings

Turning Points by Mark Noll

For additional resources go to reframecourse.com

 20 min

Engage

LN Provide tea candles for each of the participants in the group. Light the large candle, and explain that it represents the Holy Spirit. Then light each of the participants' tea candles and begin the activity. If this is not possible, then do the activity without candles and look at the photo of the candle in the guide. Please ensure that the activity is carried out safely.

ACTIVITY

The large candle represents the Holy Spirit, the light and life that sustains each of us in our faith. The Spirit empowers and sends us to carry God's light into the world. The tea candle represents your call to be a light—to bring truth and light to the world around you. As your candle is lit, notice that the flame from the large candle is not diminished, rather the light increases.

Share with one another where you want to experience more of the Holy Spirit in your life. Pray for the Holy Spirit to fill the group and send you into the world as faithful bearers of God's light.

Before the next session, pray each morning for the Holy Spirit to use you as a light to the world in ordinary, practical ways. Then, at the end of the day, pray for God to show you how the Spirit used you as a light. Record what the Spirit reveals to you in your guide or personal journal.

LN When you have finished praying, say the closing prayer for the session together. If there is anyone who speaks a language other than English, invite them to pray in that language as well.

PRAY

O Lord, who has mercy upon all, take away from me my sins, and mercifully kindle in me the fire of your Holy Spirit. Take away from me the heart of stone, and give me a heart of flesh, a heart to love and adore you, a heart to delight in you, to follow and enjoy you, for Christ's sake.
–Ambrose

Part 3: The Ongoing Story

Strangers & Exiles

PREPARE
· Review Session 8 Leader Guide
· Watch the episode and take
  note of points relevant for
  the discussion
· Pray for your group's
  time together
· Have a Bible on hand

"The task of the church is to live as resurrection people in between Easter and the final day, as a sign of the first and a foretaste of the second."

—N.T. Wright

 15 min

LN Allow for a brief time to connect and then invite the group to recall what ReFrame has covered up to this point.

LN Invite participants who completed the optional activity to share about their experience praying for the Holy Spirit to use them as a light.

LN As the recap discussion reaches a natural lull, introduce this session and then invite a participant to read aloud 2 Corinthians 5:17-20.

LN Pray for your time together and then begin the video.

Overview

RECAP

The previous five sessions explored the big chapters of the biblical story. Starting with creation and fall, then the calling of Israel, the climax in Jesus, and the ending in new heavens and earth. We live in the middle of this story. As we anticipate the story's end, the Holy Spirit pulls the church through the frame, inviting us into God's mission by seeing our vocations as part of God's work to bring shalom throughout his creation.

Since the last session, have you experienced or seen the Holy Spirit at work in your life and the wider world? If so, where?

INTRODUCTION

How do we live out this story? How do we engage the world around us? For the next two sessions, we will explore how God calls all Christians to live as ambassadors. Rather than simply assimilating or withdrawing from culture, we participate in God's mission to witness to and redeem culture.
Read 2 Corinthians 5:17-20.

40min

Episode Outline & Notes

Assimilate or Withdraw—Christians living in exile can be tempted to either assimilate or withdraw from the culture around them.

Ambassadors—Our true citizenship is in the kingdom of God, and so we are called to be ambassadors of this kingdom.

Embassy—Ambassadors need an embassy—a community in which to gather, be nurtured, and be sent from.

Church—The embassy for Christians is the local church, which gives humanity a foretaste of heaven. It is also the residence of the King of kings, Jesus Christ.

 5 min

Emmaus Road Reflection

LN When the video has finished, read Luke 24:15.

"As they talked and discussed these things with each other, Jesus himself came up and walked along with them." Luke 24:15

LN Spend five minutes in silence, praying and reflecting on the questions provided. Remind participants there is additional space in the back of the guide.

What has God been saying to me through this episode (e.g. encouragement, challenge)?

What was significant or new? What questions did it raise?

LN After this reflection time, allow for a 5-minute break.

 **40 min**

LN Don't feel pressured to cover everything. If conversation is slow, ask a starter question: what was significant, helpful, or confusing for you? What questions did it raise?

"I think as Christians we actually should be the best visionaries. We should be the people that are able to have hope in making a difference when all others are without hope because we're living in that hope of a new kingdom."

–Katherine Leary Alsdorf

Discussion

Like Fran, why do you think we are tempted to withdraw from our culture?

What are the similarities and differences between the exile we experience and the exile Daniel and the Israelites experienced? What can we learn from Daniel about engaging culture?

Where are you experiencing exile, and what difficulties do you experience there? What does it mean to be an ambassador in that place?

How is your church a local embassy? How might your church help sustain you as an ambassador? What is it doing well? What needs to change?

Further Resources

Visions of Vocation by Steven Garber

Kingdom Calling by Amy Sherman

Making the Best of It by John G. Stackhouse, Jr.

For additional resources go to reframecourse.com

15 min

LN This activity may be completed before the next session. It is a recommended, not a required activity.

Engage

ACTIVITY

God works through our vocations in the world. Think of a place where God has placed you as an ambassador, a place you know and spend time in regularly (perhaps the place you prayed for in Session 6). Before the next session, ask God to open your eyes as you go into this place or community:

- **What is good in this place that I can celebrate and cultivate?**

- **What brokenness in this place grieves me?**

As God opens your eyes to see, continue to pray for that place and ask:

- **How can I help to bring more of God's light and love—God's shalom?**

- **Who do I need to work with to do this?**

Write down what you observe and pray over it before the next session.

LN Have each person share where God has currently placed them for the majority of their week (home, community, workplace) and pray for God to help them see themselves as Christ's ambassador there. If there is time, also pray for your church as an embassy. Then close your time with the prayer for this session.

PRAY

Our Father, each day is a little life, each night a tiny death; help us to live with faith and hope and love. Lift our duty above drudgery; let not our strength fail, or the vision fade, in the heat and burden of the day. O God, make us patient and pitiful one with another in the fret and jar of life, remembering that each fights a hard fight and walks a lonely way. Forgive us, Lord, if we hurt our fellow souls; teach us a gentler tone, a sweeter charity of words, and a more healing touch. Sustain us, O God, when we must face sorrow; give us courage for the day and hope for the morrow. Day unto day may we lay hold of thy hand and look up into thy face, whatever befall, until our work is finished and the day is done. Amen.
–Francis of Assisi

Part 3: The Ongoing Story

Ambassadors

PREPARE

- Make preparations for a group meal in the final Session 10 (see LN at end of activity section)

- Review Session 9 Leader Guide

- Watch the episode and take note of points relevant for the discussion

- Pray for your group's time together

- Have a Bible on hand

"There's no hierarchy of vocations in God's kingdom. Every Christian is ultimately sent as a missionary—an ambassador of Christ—to some part of God's world."

–Paul Williams

 15 min

LN Allow for a brief time to connect and then invite the group to remember what you discussed in the previous sessions.

Overview

RECAP

The last session began an exploration of God's call for us to be ambassadors in the context of exile. As ambassadors of Christ, we need an embassy—a local church—to form and nurture us. This community acts as a foretaste of heaven and sends us into the world to participate in God's mission to redeem all of life, human beings and the creation itself.

How was the experience of seeing yourself and your vocation through the lens of an ambassador? What were you able to celebrate in the place you considered since the last session? What grieved you?

LN As the recap reaches a natural lull, introduce the session and invite a participant to read Jeremiah 29:4 –7.

INTRODUCTION

We are all called to be ambassadors, but how do we actually live as ambassadors? What does this look like? In this session, through the example of Daniel, we see that doing the diplomatic work of Christ involves being formed by the local church, knowing God's mission, learning the cultural language, and engaging in diplomacy.
Read Jeremiah 29:4-7.

LN Pray for your time together and then begin the video.

40min

Episode Outline & Notes

God calls us to be ambassadors, but how do we do this?

Establish an Ambassadorial Community—We gather with other Christians to nurture our identity in Christ and foster our missional intent.

Know the Mission—Our stories only make sense in light of God's story of his work in the world. Our vocations only make sense in light of God's vocation.

Learn the Language—Seek to understand the influences that shape our society and how the gospel speaks to them. Recognize the goodness and brokenness in the world around us.

Do the Work of Diplomacy—We act to reframe where we are in light of God's purposes and cultivate flourishing for those around us.

 5 min

Emmaus Road Reflection

LN When the video has finished, read Luke 24:15.

"As they talked and discussed these things with each other, Jesus himself came up and walked along with them." Luke 24:15

LN Spend five minutes in silence, praying and reflecting on the questions provided. Remind participants there is additional space in the back of the guide.

What has God been saying to me through this episode (e.g. encouragement, challenge)?

What was significant or new? What questions did it raise?

LN After this reflection time allow for a 5-minute break.

25min

LN Possible answers are provided in the Leader Notes, but don't feel constrained by these. Use them as a prompt if the conversation gets stuck. Once again, don't feel pressured to cover everything.

Discussion

What aspects of ambassadorship stood out for you in the stories of George Sanker (teacher) and Jennifer Wiseman (astrophysicist)?

LN Producing and selling goods and services for the well-being of his customers, members of his company, and his community.

Know the Mission: Don Flow works in the automobile industry. How did he reframe the purpose of his business from a biblical perspective?

LN To maximize profit for the owners by any means possible within the law. In practice, this can mean employees are dehumanized and not valued as being in the image of God. It can also mean that some business practices (e.g., pricing and negotiation) pursue profit unfairly by taking advantage of others.

Learn the Language: What did Don Flow identify as the dominant secular view of the purpose of business? What issues did he have with how that got worked out in practice?

LN The business used a pricing model so that everyone got a fair price regardless of gender, ethnicity, or education.

Diplomacy: How did Don change the way he practiced business within his company and with his customers?

 30 min

Engage

ACTIVITY

LN Ask for a volunteer to be the centre of a "group workshop" where the participants brainstorm answers to the questions of how we are ambassadors. If you do not have a volunteer, either suggest your own life situation or choose a job or area of life that everyone will be familiar with (e.g. accountant, lawyer, janitor, or teacher). There are no right or wrong answers; the purpose of the exercise is to practice reframing.

Christians are called to be ambassadors wherever God has placed them. How can we do this? This exercise invites you to practice, as a group, how you might engage and reframe somewhere God has placed you as an ambassador.

Context: Have someone share where God has placed them as an ambassador (e.g., the place you identified in Session 8, your workplace, neighbourhood, etc.). Once the person has shared, pray for the group: *"Lord open our eyes and imaginations to see you and your perspective in this context."*

Now brainstorm together the following questions:

Know the Mission: How could you reframe the purpose and intent of this area of life in light of God's story? Why does God care about this?

Hint: Think of themes or biblical metaphors from the course (e.g., made in the image of God, flourishing relationships with each other and creation, culture-making, creating, cultivating, people-keeping, etc.).

"We want to be the kind of company that the community wished existed if we weren't there."

—Don Flow

"For every believer, your vocation, your professional life, your family life, all of that has to be enmeshed in some sense with your following of Christ."

– Jennifer Wiseman

LN Session 10 includes the option to end ReFrame with a communal meal. Read the first Leader Note from Session 10 and ask your group how you would like to conclude your time together.

Learn the Language: How does our culture define the purpose of this area of life?

How does the purpose, and its practical outworking, relate to God's purposes? What is in alignment and good? What is out of alignment and broken? Where have we lost our way?

Hint: If you did the exercise from the last session, share your observations about what was good and what was broken with the group. Invite the group to collectively share their insights and experiences.

Diplomacy: What ideas do you have for practical changes that could bring about more of God's presence and human flourishing? What changes could be made within your sphere of influence? What changes could we advocate for at a public, corporate or institutional level?

Hint: Start by thinking about small and simple changes. What are you empowered to do? Don't feel the burden to fix everything. What can you nudge in a kingdom direction? This could be the countercultural way you treat people, speak about your work, run meetings, decorate your space, your purchasing habits, your mission statement, etc. Think about examples from stories in earlier ReFrame sessions.

Take some time before the next session to answer these questions yourself.

Further Resources

Wonder Women by Kate Harris

Taking Your Soul to Work: Overcoming the Nine Deadly Sins of the Workplace by Paul Stevens and Alvin Ung

Why Business Matters to God by Jeff Van Duzer

For additional resources go to reframecourse.com

LN Spend time praying for the sectors of society with which participants in the group have a connection (e.g. home, community, business, education, politics, media, engineering, science and technology, not-for-profit, retirement, etc.). Pray for redemption in these areas and for ambassadorial communities there. Then close your time with the prayer for this session.

PRAY

Almighty God our heavenly Father, you declare your glory and show forth your handiwork in the heavens and in the earth: deliver us in our various occupations from the service of self alone, that we may do the work you give us to do in truth and beauty and for the common good; for the sake of him who came among us as one who serves, your Son Jesus Christ our Lord, who lives and reigns with you and the Holy Spirit, one God, for ever and ever. Amen.
–"For Vocation in Daily Work" from the *Book of Common Prayer*

Part 3: The Ongoing Story

Joyful Living

PREPARE

- If applicable prepare for the meal
- Review Session 10 Leader Guide
- Watch the episode and take note of points relevant for the discussion
- Pray for your group's time together
- Have a Bible on hand

"As I grew closer to Jesus, following him into my calling, what I discover is this joy that the world can't take away. And so I don't necessarily have success. I don't necessarily have recognition. But I do have joy that nothing can take away."

-Andy Crouch

 **15 min**

Overview

LN This is an optional activity, but it is recommended that you celebrate the conclusion of ReFrame and your time together with a meal. This could happen before the session begins, with participants contributing to the meal. If a meal is not possible, consider providing snacks or a dessert for the group to share during the session.

RECAP

If Jesus is the redeemer of all things, what does this mean for every aspect of our lives? This is the question ReFrame has explored. The full scriptural story opens our eyes to see and encounter Jesus more clearly in every area of life. Only when we know the story and understand ourselves as ambassadors of Christ's good news can we live reframed lives and faithfully participate in God's big story of redemption.

What ways have you been exploring the vocation of an ambassador of Christ since the last session?

LN Allow for a brief time to connect and then invite the group to recall what ReFrame has covered up to this point.

INTRODUCTION

A reframed understanding of the gospel gives confidence and joy in the midst of daily life. The good news of Christ in the Scriptures frees us for an abundant life of work and rest. **Read Luke 24:30-32.**

LN As the recap reaches a natural lull, introduce the session and invite a participant to read Luke 24:30-32.

LN Pray for your time together and then begin the video.

40min

Episode Outline & Notes

The story of the disciples' encounter with Jesus on the road to Emmaus takes the following shape:

Encounter—Jesus encounters us in the midst of our fragmentation and confusion.

Understand—Jesus reframes our understanding of ourselves, and the world, by explaining the biblical story.

Respond—We can live with joy and confidence as Christ's ambassadors.

 5 min

LN When the video has finished, read Luke 24:15.

LN Spend five minutes in silence, praying and reflecting on the questions provided. Remind participants there is additional space in the back of the guide.

LN After this reflection time, allow for a 5-minute break. Since this is the final session of ReFrame, consider asking the participants to use their Emmaus Road reflections to engage some of the discussion questions.

Emmaus Road Reflection

"As they talked and discussed these things with each other, Jesus himself came up and walked along with them." Luke 24:15

What has God been saying to me through this episode (e.g. encouragement, challenge)?

What was significant or new? What questions did it raise?

 **40 min**

LN Don't feel pressured to cover everything. If conversation is slow to get going ask a starter question: what was significant, helpful, or confusing for you?

Discussion

What does joy and confidence look like in the midst of the sorrows, heartaches, and disappointments of life— not only yours but of the wider world? In what do we place our trust and hope?

What have you seen with fresh eyes during ReFrame? What questions are you still wrestling with?

What sustains us as ambassadors on our journey of discipleship?

What is God saying to you, your church, and your community about how you can be an ambassador to the culture around you?

Further Resources

A Long Obedience in the Same Direction by Eugene Peterson

Keeping the Sabbath Wholly by Marva Dawn

The World Is Not Ours to Save by Tyler Wigg-Stevenson

For additional resources go to reframecourse.com

"It's all of Grace. So to live in Christ is to live a gracious life, and to live in grace means you are always living in gratitude."

–Jim Houston

 5 min

LN End ReFrame by praying for God to help you live as joyful ambassadors of Christ. Then close your time by saying the prayer for this session together.

Engage

PRAY

Leader to life, Path to truth, our Lord Jesus Christ; you led Joseph to Egypt, and the people of Israel through the Red Sea; and Moses to Mount Sinai, and his people to the land of promise. And you traveled with Cleopas and his companion to Emmaus. Now, I pray you, Lord lead me and my companions to travel in peace on the journey before us. Save us from the visible and invisible enemy and lead us safely to the place we are headed. For you are our way and our truth and our life. Glory and worship to you now and always and unto the ages of ages. Amen.
–Hovhannes Garnets'i

Continuing
the Journey

Having completed ReFrame, what shape will your ongoing journey take? These next pages offer a few suggestions.

Encounter Jesus in the everyday

Pray. End each day with a prayer. Where have I encountered Christ in my life, work, and relationships today? Are there places of frustration or pain in which I need to ask Jesus to meet me?

Gather. During the week, gather a group of two or three to pray into the challenges and opportunities you're encountering as you seek to live out your faith in all of life.

Participate in Christ's mission in the world

Get involved. What's going on in your local church? Commit to an existing program or project.

Start a missional community. Are there others in your church, workplace, or neighbourhood with a common vision to participate in Christ's renewing work in the world? Gather together to seek God for concrete ways to engage, and combine your efforts for greater impact.

Share ReFrame. Are there others who would benefit from participating in ReFrame? Tell them about the resource or even lead a course yourself.

Deepen your understanding of Jesus' work in the world

THE WASHINGTON INSTITUTE

The Washington Institute helps individuals and institutions recover a deeper understanding of vocation through a range of articles, mentorship, and retreats, as well as through consulting with companies, organizations, and institutions.
washingtoninst.org

REGENT COLLEGE

Regent College, a graduate school of theology in Vancouver, Canada, provides a range of learning opportunities for people seeking to live out their faith in all of life.

MARKETPLACE INSTITUTE—Provides curriculum, events, and other resources designed to equip people to live as Christ's ambassador in their daily work with particular interest in business, science, politics, and the environment.
rgnt.net/marketplace

REGENT AUDIO—Listen to intelligent, thought-provoking, and vibrant theological audio from Regent College faculty and other world-renowned theologians. Learn on-the-go about science and faith, arts, Bible, marketplace, history, ethical and social issues, and more in mp3 download or DVD format.
rgnt.net/audio

SUMMER PROGRAMS—The most extensive theological summer program in the world, with intensive one- to two-week courses taught in Vancouver, Canada, by leading theologians and professors from around the globe. Summer courses are a great way to deepen your theological understanding without the rigours of a regular academic term.
rgnt.net/summer

GRADUATE DEGREE PROGRAMS—Designed to prepare you to live out your God-given vocation, immerse you in a diverse community of believers, and equip you to engage thoughtfully and intelligently with the wider culture. Choose from a range of Masters degree programs that can be completed through a combination of in-residence and distance education courses.
rgnt.net/programs

Prayers Throughout the Ages

SESSION 1 & 10

Leader to life, Path to truth, our Lord Jesus Christ; You led Joseph to Egypt, and the people of Israel through the Red Sea; And Moses to Mount Sinai, And his people to the land of promise. And you traveled with Cleopas and his companion to Emmaus. Now, I pray you, Lord lead me and my companions to travel in peace on the journey before us. Save us from the visible and invisible enemy and lead us safely to the place we are headed. For you are our way and our truth and our life. Glory and worship to you now and always and unto the ages of ages. Amen. –*Hovhannes Garnets'i*

BIO Hovhannes Garnets'i (c. 1180-1245) was an Armenian monk and hermit.

SESSION 2

Lord, to be turned from you is to fall, to be turned to you is to rise, and to stand in you is to abide forever. Grant us in all our duties your help, in all our perplexities your guidance, in all our dangers your protection, and in all our sorrow your peace; through Jesus Christ our Lord. –*Augustine*

BIO Augustine (354-430) was a pastor, theologian, and bishop of Hippo Regius (present-day Annaba, Algeria).

SESSION 3

Give us grace, O Lord, to work while it is day, fulfilling diligently and patiently whatever duty you appoint us to do; doing small things in the day of small things, and great labors if you summon us to any; rising and working, sitting still and suffering, according to thy word. God with us, and we will go, but if you do not go with us, send us not; go before us, if you put us forth; let us hear thy voice when we follow. Hear us, we beseech you, for the glory of your great name.
–*Christina Rossetti*

BIO Christina Rossetti (1830-1894) was an English devotional writer and poet.

SESSION 4

God, you called your servant Abraham from Ur in Chaldea, watching over him in all his wanderings, and guided the Hebrew people as they crossed the desert. Guide and guard us your children who, for the love of your name, journey through this life. Be our companion on the way, our guide at the crossroads, our strength in weariness, our defense in dangers, our shelter on the path, our shade in the heat, our light in the darkness, our comfort in discouragement; that through your guidance, we may arrive safely at the end of our journey and, enriched with grace and truth, may return to our homes filled with lasting joy. –*Codex Calixtinus*

BIO The Codex Calixtinus is an illustrated manuscript from the 12th century that includes sermons, songs, and advice for pilgrims traveling the Way of St. James (*El Camino de Santiago*).

SESSION 5

Christ be with me, Christ within me,
Christ behind me, Christ before me,
Christ beside me, Christ to win me,
Christ to comfort and restore me,
Christ beneath me, Christ above me,
Christ in quiet, Christ in danger,
Christ in hearts of all that love me,
Christ in mouth of friend and stranger.
–*Patrick*

BIO Patrick (387-461) was a missionary and bishop to the Celtic people of Ireland.

SESSION 6

"God of heaven and earth, we pray for your kingdom to come, for your will to be done on earth as it is in heaven. Teach us to see our vocations and occupations as woven into your work in the world. We ask for your great mercy, for ourselves and those around us. Give us eyes to see that our work is holy to you, O Lord, even as our worship is holy to you. In the name of the Father, Son and Holy Spirit. Amen." *–Steven Garber*

BIO Steven Garber is a teacher, writer and founding principal of The Washington Institute For Faith, Vocation & Culture.

Adapted from *Visions of Vocation* by Steven Garber. Copyright (c) 2014 by Steven Garber. Used by permission of InterVarsity Press, P.O. Box 1400, Downers Grove, IL 60515, USA. www.ivpress.com

SESSION 7

O Lord, who has mercy upon all, take away from me my sins, and mercifully kindle in me the fire of your Holy Spirit. Take away from me the heart of stone, and give me a heart of flesh, a heart to love and adore you, a heart to delight in you, to follow and enjoy you, for Christ's sake. *–Ambrose*

BIO Ambrose (340-397) was archbishop of Milan and a key figure during the Arian controversy.

SESSION 8

Our Father, each day is a little life, each night a tiny death; help us to live with faith and hope and love. Lift our duty above drudgery; let not our strength fail, or the vision fade, in the heat and burden of the day. O God, make us patient and pitiful one with another in the fret and jar of life, remembering that each fights a hard fight and walks a lonely way. Forgive us, Lord, if we hurt our fellow souls; teach us a gentler tone, a sweeter charity of words, and a more healing touch. Sustain us, O God, when we must face sorrow; give us courage for the day and hope for the morrow. Day unto day may we lay hold of thy hand and look up into thy face, whatever befall, until our work is finished and the day is done. Amen. *–Francis of Assisi*

BIO Francis of Assisi (1181-1226) was a Catholic friar, priest, and founder of the Franciscan Order.

SESSION 9

Almighty God our heavenly Father, you declare your glory and show forth your handiwork in the heavens and in the earth: deliver us in our various occupations from the service of self alone, that we may do the work you give us to do in truth and beauty and for the common good; for the sake of him who came among us as one who serves, your Son Jesus Christ our Lord, who lives and reigns with you and the Holy Spirit, one God, for ever and ever. Amen. –*"For Vocation in Daily Work"* from the *Book of Common Prayer*

BIO *The Book of Common Prayer* is the prayer book of the Anglican Communion originally published in 1549.

Editor note: *some prayers have been edited and updated for contemporary language.*

Speaker Biographies

Presenters

MARK MAYHEW

Mark Mayhew is the co-creator of ReFrame, faculty associate at Regent College and former director of the Regent College Marketplace Institute. Mark is passionate about helping people integrate Christian faith with the whole of life. Prior to graduate theological training, his background was in business consulting, where he worked across multiple industry sectors.

ERIN ANTOSH

Erin Antosh is Director of Programs and Development at The Washington Institute for Faith, Vocation, and Culture. She loves knowing that God is involved in, and deeply cares about, all aspects of our lives. Erin moved to Washington, D.C. in 2006 to participate in the Falls Church Fellows Program and has since worked in national politics in policy, communications and fundraising positions.

Speakers

PAUL WILLIAMS | Sessions 1, 8 & 9

Paul Williams is Executive Director of the Marketplace Institute and the David J. Brown Family Associate Professor of Marketplace, Theology, and Leadership at Regent College. He previously served as Chief Economist and Head of International Research for an international real estate consulting and investment banking group based in London, England. His research and writing has focused on the relationship of Christian faith to contemporary economic life.

SARAH WILLIAMS | Session 2

Sarah Williams is Associate Professor of the History of Christianity at Regent College. She is a specialist in modern British social and cultural history and previously taught at the University of Oxford. She is the author of *Religious Belief and Popular Culture* and co-author of *Redefining Christian Britain*.

IAIN PROVAN | Session 3

Iain Provan is the Marshall Sheppard Professor of Biblical Studies at Regent College and is also an ordained minister of the Church of Scotland. One of the world's experts on Israelite history, he previously taught at London and Edinburgh universities. He has recently published two books: *Convenient Myths and Seriously Dangerous Religion*.

PHIL LONG | Session 4

Phil Long is Professor of Old Testament at Regent College. Prior to Regent, he taught for fifteen years at Covenant Theological Seminary in Missouri and four years at the Freie Theologische Akademie in Germany. He has published several books on biblical history, including the co-authored work *A Biblical History of Israel* and a commentary on 1 and 2 Samuel in the *ESV Study Bible*.

RIKK WATTS | Sessions 5 & 6

Rikk Watts is Professor of New Testament at Regent College. He was trained as an aeronautical engineer and worked for IBM while undertaking a degree in philosophy, art history, and sociology. Rikk is an expert on the relationship of the Old and New Testaments and heads the "Mark" section of the Society of Biblical Literature. He is the author of *Isaiah's New Exodus in Mark*.

BRUCE HINDMARSH | Session 7

Bruce Hindmarsh is the James M. Houston Professor of Spiritual Theology at Regent College and an expert on the history of evangelical piety. He is the author of *John Newton and the English Evangelical Tradition* and *The Evangelical Conversion Narrative*. In 2012, he was elected President of the American Society of Church History—the first time a non-American was awarded this post.

POLLY LONG | Session 10

Polly Long is a sessional lecturer at Regent College. She teaches Greek and has led numerous seminars on homiletics and studying the Bible. Polly has initiated evangelistic outreaches to women in the US, Germany, England, and Canada, and was involved at the founding level of a ministry to women who have been sexually exploited through prostitution in Vancouver, British Columbia.

Note: *Bios for additional contributors can be found at reframecourse.com*

Notes

Space for additional notes, reflections, sketches.

"As they talked and discussed these things with each other, Jesus himself came up and walked along with them."
Luke 24:15

CPSIA information can be obtained
at www.ICGtesting.com
Printed in the USA
BVOW07s0010040317

477753BV00001B/1/P